THE ADVENTURE ZONE

Here There Be Gerblins

Based on the podcast by

Griffin McElroy   Clint McElroy

Travis McElroy   Justin McElroy

Adaptation by

Clint McElroy   Carey Pietsch

Art by

Carey Pietsch

:01

First Second

New York

First Second

Text copyright © 2018 by Clint McElroy, Griffin McElroy, Justin McElroy, Travis McElroy
Illustrations copyright © 2018 by Carey Pietsch
Letterer: Tess Stone
Flatters: Niki Smith, Megan Brennan

Fan art gallery copyright © 2018 by (respectively):
Annie Clementine Johnston-Glick
Jonah Matteo Baumann
Cheyanne Bueno
Chris Kindred
Liz Parlett
Michael Mayne
Sebastián Jimenez
Mickey Quinn
Mu X. Jones
Johanna The Mad
Adrienne Valdes

Published by First Second
First Second is an imprint of Roaring Brook Press, a division
of Holtzbrinck Publishing Holdings Limited Partnership
175 Fifth Avenue, New York, NY 10010
All rights reserved

Library of Congress Control Number: 2017946143

ISBN: 978-1-250-15370-8
ISBN: 978-1-250-19784-9 (B&N Edition)
ISBN: 978-1-250-19895-2 (Special Edition)

Our books may be purchased in bulk for promotional, educational, or business use.
Please contact your local bookseller or the Macmillan Corporate and Premium Sales Department
at (800) 221-7945 ext. 5442 or by e-mail at MacmillanSpecialMarkets@macmillan.com.

FIRST
EDITION

First edition, 2018
Book design by Andrew Arnold
Printed in the Unied States of America

Penciled with a 2B pencil-style tool in Photoshop. Inked with a brush-style
digital nib in Clip Studio Paint and colored digitally in Photoshop.

5 7 9 10 8 6

Introduction

When it comes to *The Adventure Zone,* and the McElroys as a whole, I'll admit that I've been late to the game.

My friends have adored them for years. But I'm stubborn, so it wasn't until November of 2016 that I finally caved to peer pressure and began sampling their unique flavor of artisanal auditory delectation.

I listened to an episode of *My Brother, My Brother and Me,* and the McElroys hit my life like a new religion. Within two months I'd listened to more than 250 episodes of *MBMBaM.* And I would have made it through the entirety of their archive shortly thereafter . . .

. . . but then I discovered *The Adventure Zone.*

If learning about *MBMBaM* was like a religious conversion, *The Adventure Zone* was like suddenly falling in love. Plus getting hit by lightning. Plus coffee. Plus hugging Lin-Manuel Miranda while eating an ice-cream sundae.

Okay. I'm not doing a good job of this. Let me start again.

For those of you who may not know, I'm a fantasy author. My books have been translated into thirty-five languages and sell millions of copies all over the world. I mention this not to brag, but because it's the easiest way to prove I know a little bit about stories. I story for a living. I'm pretty good at it.

So let me say, honestly and sincerely, that *The Adventure Zone* is some of the finest storytelling I have ever experienced. In any genre. Ever.

I also know a little bit about role-playing. I've played D&D since 1982. Worked my way through every edition. (Except 4th.) These days I play D&D in packed stadiums with Acquisitions Incorporated. I guest star in *Critical Role.* I've visited the D&D offices, and we're currently working on some secret collaborations together.

With that in mind, I'd like to say that the McElroys have done something with D&D I have never seen before. They've done something I didn't know it was possible to do. They've made something magical, and loving, and kind, and beautiful. The world is better because this story is in it.

I've listened to the entirety of *The Adventure Zone* more than three times over the last eight months. I'm not just a fan, I'm a missionary. I'm a zealot. I'm not saying I'm working on my Merle cosplay or anything . . . But yeah. Fine. I'll admit it, I'm working on my cosplay.

What you hold in your hands is a unique experiment. A brave, even remarkable thing. This comic is an attempt to translate pure audio improvisational storytelling into a visual medium. I've done some work in comics, and I can't think of a harder transition for a story to make.

And I adore what the McElroys and their brilliant collaborator— co-adaptor and artist Carey Pietsch—have done here. Not just in the reflected light of my affection for *The Adventure Zone* podcast, but as an entity distinct unto itself. I already know the story, but there are surprises here. I know what's going to happen, but I love seeing these good, good boys beginning their marvelous adventure all over again.

—Pat Rothfuss
November 2017

Chapter 1

I'M VERY CONFLICTED! I DON'T TRUST THIS BOGARD GUY!

HE *HIRED* US FOR THIS JOB! AND HE'S YOUR COUSIN!

EXACTLY! I KNOW HIM PRETTY WELL!

IF IT WEREN'T FOR ME, HE'D BE THE BIGGEST ASSHOLE IN OUR FAMILY.

AND THAT SO-CALLED "BODYGUARD," BARRY, AIN'T NO DAY AT THE BEACH, EITHER.

WHY DIDN'T THEY JUST TAKE ALL THIS WITH THEM INSTEAD OF HAVING US HAUL IT?

I CAN'T FIND ANYTHING EDIBLE, THAT'S FOR SURE.

A BUNCH OF MINING STUFF, SHIT TO BLOW UP OTHER SHIT.

THE ONLY MINE IN THESE PARTS WAS LOST A DECADE AGO.

AND THE WAY YOUR COUSIN KEPT SAYING "THIS IS THE LAST JOB YOU'LL EVER NEED! THE *LAST JOB* YOU'LL *EVER NEED!*"

I GET THE WHOLE "WINK-WINK YOU'RE GONNA BE RICH" VIBE, BUT IT CAME ACROSS AS KIND OF MURDER-Y.

I AM... UNEASY.

THEN YOU ARE JUST GONNA *LOVE* THIS.

IT'S KIND OF TOUGH TO SEE...

...BUT I THINK THE SHIT HAS GONE SOUTH.

YOU GUYS JUST WON YOUR FIRST FIGHT! WITH FUCKING *APLOMB!*

THEY NEVER EVEN TOUCHED US! I ALMOST FEEL BAD.

ONE KILL EACH!

WE SHOULD LOOT THE DEAD GERBLINS!

WHICH ONE YOU GONNA LOOT THERE, SPARKY?

THE FLASH-FROZEN ONE IN A MILLION PIECES? THE ONE CUT IN HALF AND COVERED WITH GOO?

OR THE ONE LOST IN THE WEEDS?

I SHOULD AT LEAST TAKE THIS PRETTY SWEET BOW, RIGHT?

AFTER ALL, I HAVE A PROFICIENCY IN RANGED WEAPONS.

OF *COURSE* YOU DO.

HERE, DWARF. I FOUND YOUR GROSS AX IN THE GERBLIN YOU MERCILESSLY KILLED.

FIND ANYTHING ELSE, FRIEND TAAKO?

TWANG!

NOPE. NOTHING. NOT A THING, FRIEND MAGNUS.

THEN WE SHOULD INSPECT WHERE THE ATTACK TOOK PLACE!

LET US NOT TARRY!

I'M WITH YOU, MY MAN! I AM ALWAYS ANTI-TARRYING!

STILL WARM. THIS DIDN'T HAPPEN VERY LONG AGO.

NO BOGARD, NO BARRY, AND NO MAP.

AND WHAT THE HELL DID HE NEED A MAP FOR? HE KNOWS THE WAY TO HAVERDALE!

SO WHAT DO WE DO NOW?

"AND THAT WAS THE SAD, BORING END OF THEIR FIRST MISSION!"

I THINK THIS CHANGES THINGS!

IT MAKES NO SENSE TO DELIVER THE WAGON TO HAVERDALE IF BOGARD ISN'T EVEN THERE.

BUT WE DON'T KNOW **WHERE** HE IS!

IF YOU GUYS ARE DONE...

...WE COULD JUST FOLLOW THOSE DRAG MARKS INTO THE BRUSH?

MAGNUS RUSHES HEADLONG INTO THE BRUSH!

WAIT! WHAT ABOUT OUR STUFF?!

OH, DON'T **WORRY**, MAGNUS! WE'LL TAKE CARE OF **EVERYTHING!!**

YOU JUST RUN OFF AND LEAVE US TO TAKE CARE OF THE WAGON! TOTALLY COOL! SUPER COOL.

COOL, THANKS, BYE!

SNAARRL GROWL

THAT SOUNDS LIKE...WOLVES?

KLANK KLI CHANK

AND A LOT OF SCARY CHAINS.

KLUNK KA-CHUNK

YOU GUYS DO REALIZE THAT'S KIND OF THE WAY THIS WORKS, RIGHT? I FILL A CHAMBER WITH SCARY SHIT, AND YOU FIGHT IT.

ALL RIGHT, FELLAS. LET'S THINK ABOUT THIS...

MAGNUS BELIEVES THINKING IS FOR OTHER PEOPLE!

HE TENDS MORE TOWARD—

—ACTION!!

I GUESS WE SHOULD GO AFTER HIM...?

NAH.

TAAKO'S GOOD OUT HERE.

"GO TO HAVERDALE. DELIVER A WAGON. HAVE A FEW LAUGHS."

I SHOULD HAVE STAYED ON THE BEACH.

—AND THEN THE LIGHTS COME UP, AND THERE I AM,

STANDING UNDER A MAGNIFICENT BANNER THAT READS:

SIZZLE IT UP WITH TAAKO!

SO, IT'S A SHOW...ABOUT COOKING?

IT'S ABOUT *LIFE!*

MMMRR??

GRRRRRR!

...TOLD THROUGH THE PERSPECTIVE OF FINE DINING.

RRRRRAR SNAAAR

RRLLL

WELL... THAT SOUNDS...

GRRARGH!!

CRASH

...NIFTY.

CLATTER CLUNK

TAP TAP TAP TAP

SO! HOW WAS THE OMINOUS CLANKING CAVERN?

TAP TAP

I DON'T WANT TO TALK ABOUT IT.

THAT'S OKAY,

I REALLY DIDN'T GIVE A SHIT.

17

HECKIE DARN. CAVE-IN. CAN'T GET THROUGH THAT.

OH, WELL. MISSION OVER. WE GAVE IT A GOOD SHOT—

NOT SO FAST.

WITH MY REMARKABLE UPPER-BODY STRENGTH, I CAN HAVE THOSE ROCKS MOVED IN...THREE DAYS, TOPS.

ORRRRRR—

I GOT YOUR "PERCEPTION CHECK" RIGHT HERE.

HELLO, FRIEND!!

WHO'S DOWN THERE?

HOWDY, NEIGHBOR!

WE'RE EXPLORERS! WE'VE TAKEN A WRONG TURN!

YOU CERTAINLY *HAVE.*

I WOULD ACTUALLY *HEARTILY* RECOMMEND YOU TURN AROUND. THIS IS NOT A GREAT PLACE FOR TOURISM.

WE MEAN YOU NO HARM, BUT I WOULD *NOT* SUGGEST LAUNCHING AN ATTACK ON US!

WE'RE *VERY* DANGEROUS!

OH?

EXACTLY HOW DANGEROUS ARE WE TALKING?

LEVEL... LEVEL ONE?

OR... HIGHER...

LOOOOK, MY DUDE...I THINK WE'VE GOTTEN OFF ON THE WRONG—

GO ASK THE GERBLIN WE CUT IN *HALF* HOW DANGEROUS WE ARE!

OH, EXCELLENT! I WAS JUST STARTING TO ESTABLISH A RAPPORT!

WELL PLAYED!

TO BE FAIR, HE WASN'T AS COOL AS YOU ARE!

I'M PICKING UP ON A REAL AGGRESSIVE VIBE FROM DOWN THERE.

HERE YOU ARE IN OUR HIDEOUT.

I DON'T KNOW WHO YOU ARE OR WHAT YOU'RE DOING.

YOU ARE MAKING ME ANXIOUS.

I'M... *UNPLEASANT* WHEN I'M ANXIOUS.

CAST A SPELL...THAT WILL PUSH HIM...OFF... THE...BRIDGE.

EVERYTHING'S CHILL, MY DUDE.

WE'RE LOOKING FOR A FRIEND OF OURS? HE WAS TAKEN AND HIS HORSES WERE KILLED?

PUSH... HIM... OFF!

YEAH, WE DID THAT.

IS THERE A PROBLEM?

HEY, SID! THERE ARE SOME GUYS HERE ABOUT THE DEAD HORSES!

HORSES?

THE ONES WE SHOT.

OH, RIGHT! GOOD TIMES.

LET'S GET CRANKIN'!

CRANK

CRANK

KLAAANGG

rrrruummblee

THAT'S DISCONCERTING.

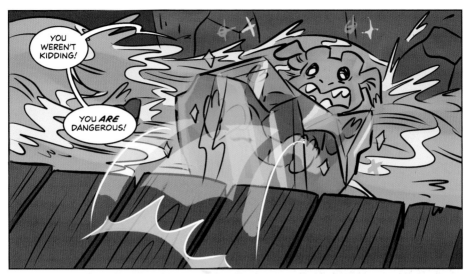

EVERYTHING'S GOOD!

YOU GUYS GO AHEAD! TAA—

ahem

—*JEFF* IS GOOD OUT HERE!

BE SURE TO GRAB SOMETHING TO SHOW G'NASH!

MANAGEMENT IS REALLY PUTTING THE HEAT ON US TO BRING IN MORE BATTLE TROPHIES!

SURE, SURE! I'LL CHOP OFF THEIR FEET AND BRING THEM!

DAMN, JEFF!

I JUST MEANT A WATCH OR SOMETHING!

YOU'VE GOTTEN SO DARK SINCE YOU BROKE UP WITH MARLENE!

YOU REALLY NEED TO TALK TO SOMEBODY!

EMBARRASSING, THIS IS.

I FEEL LOUSY. LIKE I'M DOWN TO THREE HIT POINTS.

I NEED TO TAKE A KNEE AFTER HAULING YOUR SORRY ASS UP THE WALL.

SNIFF—

IS THAT...

SNIFF SNIFF—

...ROASTING MEAT?

I KNOW THAT SMELL!!

THAT'S MY RECIPE FOR HAUNCH Á LA TAAKO!!

IT WAS IN MY VERY FIRST COOKBOOK!

Perfection:

COOK the TAAKO WAY

YOU KIDS CATCH YOUR BREATH. I GOTTA CHECK THIS OUT.

THAT, MY DUDES, IS TRUE HAUTE CUISINE!

GFOOSH

I JUST HOPE IT ISN'T HOT COUSIN.

Chapter 2

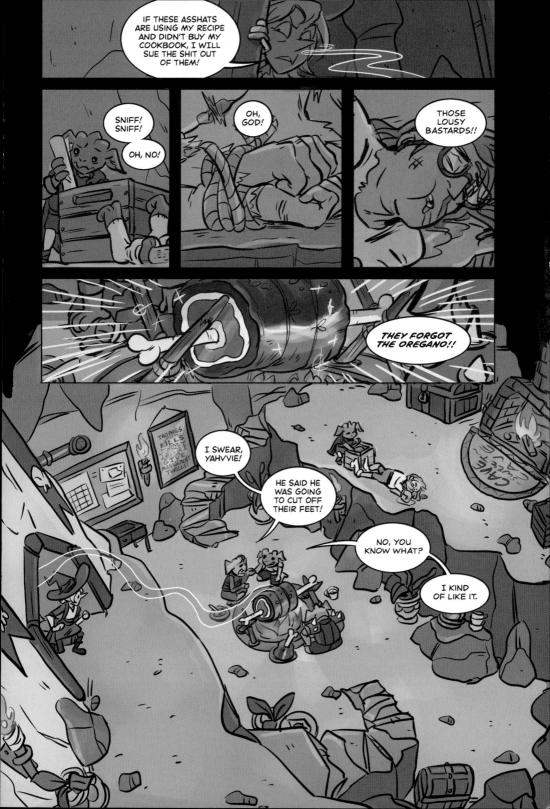

HUDDLE

I SHOULD RUN UP THE STAIRWAY AND VALIANTLY RESCUE BARRY.

I'LL GET THE GUARD UP TOP.

AND *I'LL* SKRAG THE THREE AT THE CAMPFIRE.

I'M THINKING THE DUDE DUDE IS BARRY WHAT'S-HIS-NAME THAT YOUR COUSIN WAS TALKING ABOUT.

ALL THREE?

HEY, WE'RE FOUR-AND-OH AGAINST THESE DICKHEADS!

PIECE OF CAKE.

I DON'T SEE WHAT WE GET OUT OF THIS.

WE HAVE TO FIND BOGARD, AND WE NEED THIS BARRY BLUEJEANS GUY TO DO IT.

BUT—

EVERYONE NEEDS A BARRY BLUEJEANS!!

WE'RE NOT TALKING TO YOU!

VERY WELL, YAKOV—

YAHVVIE.

YAHVVIE. WE ARE ALL IN ONE ACCORD—

NO WE'RE NOT!

WE WILL TAKE CARE OF THIS..."G'NASH"... FOR YOU.

OH, HOW PEACHY.

HE'S JUST RIGHT ACROSS THE OVERPASS.

GOODBYE!

HAVE FUN!!

ENJOY YOUR MURDER SPREE!

GUYS, I THINK THIS MIGHT BE A TRAP.

YEAH, WELL, NO SHIT!

GOOD. JUST SO WE'RE ON THE SAME PAGE.

BUT...

WE'RE STILL GONNA DO IT?

BUMP!!

dodge!

YUP.

FIRST WE TAKE CARE OF THIS G'NASH GUY...

THEN GO BACK AND GET YAHVVIE?

OH, YEAH, MY DUDE—

—WE'RE KILLIN' EVERYBODY.

I COULD USE THAT SPELL I USED BEFORE TO ILLUMINATE THE AX. YOU KNOW... SPECIAL EFFECTS.

A *LIGHT* SPELL?

YOU THINK THIS DUDE'S NEVER SEEN *LIGHT* BEFORE?

I MEAN, IF SOMETHING ALL OF A SUDDEN STARTS TO GLOW—

THAT'S WHAT THEY TEACH KIDS.

THEY TEACH LIGHT IN KINDERGARTEN.

NO, I THINK THIS IS A GOOD IDEA!

AND AT THE SAME TIME I'LL PRESTIDIGITATE ONE OF THOSE CANTRIP THINGS AND MAKE A SHOWER OF SPARKS.

AND *I'LL* BUILD A CHAIR WITH MY CARPENTRY TOOLS!

ORRRRR, YOU COULD DRAW A BEAD ON THIS G'NASH DUDE WITH YOUR BOW.

UNLESS... UNLESS HE DOESN'T FEEL THREATENED BY US, BECAUSE WE'RE ONLY LEVEL ONE.

THAT'S WHY WE'RE FIRING OFF THE FIREWORKS AND THE LIGHT!

LET'S GET TRUCKIN'!

I LOVE IT WHEN WE PLAN SHIT.

DO YOU GUYS NEED ANY MONEY? CAN I JUST SORT OF GIVE YOU EVERYTHING I HAVE?

OH, NO, NOOOOO.

MAYBE SOME OOLONG?

NO TIME FOR THAT. THE CHARM PERSON SPELL I ZAPPED YOU WITH ONLY LASTS AN HOUR.

WE HAVE A BIT OF A SITCH WE WANTED TO LOOP YOU IN ON.

ONE OF YOUR EMPLOYEES, I THINK HIS NAME IS YANNI...?

I DON'T THINK I EMPLOY ANY INTERNATIONALLY ADORED KEYBOARDISTS WITH AWESOME HAIR.

I THINK IT'S WEE-MAN.

I THINK IT'S MEEMAW.

OH! DO YOU MEAN—

JEEZ, THAT LOOKS LIKE ABOUT 19 DAMAGE.

MUST HURT LIKE A SUMBITCH

YAHVVIE?

YES! THAT'S IT! YAHVVIE!

GOOD OLE YAHVVIE. HE WAS "HENCHMAN OF THE MONTH" IN FEBRUARY.

YOU FELLAS SURE YOU DON'T WANT SOME TEA? I HAVE A WONDERFUL EARL GREY—

FIFTY-EIGHT MINUTES, G'NASH. TRY TO STAY FOCUSED.

SNAP! SNAP!

SO, YAHVVIE, HUH? HE'S PRETTY SPECIAL, ISN'T HE?

YOUR BUDDY YEEHAW IS HOLDING BARRY BLUEJEANS CAPTIVE.

OH, YES! BARRY! WONDERFUL FELLOW! VERY CORDIAL!

UNTIL YOU BEAT HIM WITHIN AN INCH OF HIS LIFE...?

OOOH, YES. SORRY ABOUT THAT.

WATER UNDER THE BRIDGE, MY GOOD MAN.

THIS YABBO OF YOURS—

YAHVVIE.

RIGHT. YERTLE SAID HE WOULD RELEASE BARRY TO US IF WE...

...THIS IS GONNA BE TOUGH TO HEAR...

HE SAID—

MUNCH

'E SAID 'EE 'OTTA 'ILL '00.

'EEDS OREGA'O.

GOOD HEAVENS! YOU'RE NOT GOING TO KILL ME, ARE YOU, TAAKO?

HELL, NO! WE'RE *BEST BUDS!*

ARE YOU SURE IT'S YAHVVIE? THERE'S A YORICK THAT WORKS FOR ME, AND HE'S ALWAYS BEEN A PAIN.

HEY! HEYYYYY! LOOK AT ME. LOOK AT THIS FACE!

IT'S TAAKO. THIS IS TAAKO TALKING. WOULD I LIE TO YOU?

ALL WE WANT YOU TO DO IS HELP US KILL YAHVVIE.

AND GET BARRY BLUEJEANS BACK FOR US.

AND TELL US WHAT HAPPENED TO OUR OTHER FRIEND, BOGARD.

AND MAYBE GIVE US A LITTLE GOLD.

MAYBE A MODERATE AMOUNT OF GOLD.

OR A LOT.

IT'S REALLY WHATEVER YOU FEEL COMFORTABLE WITH.

WHAT DO YOU SAY, FRIEND G'NASH?

I SAY WE WILL CLEAR UP THIS MATTER SPIT-SPOT.

HELLO? HELLO? TESTING, TESTING?

YAHVVIE, MAY I SEE YOU IN MY OFFICE, PLEASE?

I THINK ONCE YAHVVIE HAS A CHANCE TO AIR HIS GRIEVANCES, WE CAN RESOLVE THE WHOLE UNPLEASANT INCIDENT.

THIS IS SOME REALLY GOOD WORK! NICE FERRULES.

AS SOON AS HE SEES US, HE'S GONNA KNOW SOMETHING'S UP.

I'M TELLING YOU FELLOWS— THERE'S NO NEED FOR ALL THIS WORRY!

HE TALKS A BIG GAME, BUT YAHVVIE REALLY IS AS SWEET AS CHERRY PIE.

WE COULD PRETEND WE'RE CAPTIVES! OR PRETEND WE'RE DEAD!

I LIKE IT!

YAHVVIE!

Chapter 3

BOY! I WISH I HADN'T NEEDED TO MURDER THEM.

YES, YES, VERY SAD.

I GUESS I SHOULD HAVE SUSPECTED SOMETHING.

HE WAS A BIT CROSS AFTER HIS LAST JOB REVIEW.

DON'T BLAME YOURSELF.

PAT PAT

LISTEN, G'NASH, I'M GOING TO HAVE TO SEARCH THEM...FOR VALUABLES.

YOU KNOW... PROCEDURE.

WELL, I... SUPPOSE SO?

AND ANY VALUABLES *YOU* DON'T MIND PARTING WITH?

WHY DO I FIND THAT GUY SO DAMNED CHARMING?

THIRTY GOLD PIECES FOR THE TAAKO BENEVOLENT FUND.

YEAH, WELL, IF YOU ARE GOING TO DO ANY MORE PILFERING, MAKE IT QUICK.

I THINK YOUR CHARM SPELL IS WEARING OFF.

LET'S GET BACK TO BARRY BLUEJEANS.

BEFORE TEATIME? NEVER!

BUT YOU JUST SAID THERE WASN'T TIME FOR–

THAT WAS BEFORE I GOT VERY VERY THIRSTY...

...FOR TEA.

DID SOMEONE SAY TEATIME?!

AND VALUABLES, YES.

G'NASH, SINCE WE'RE FRIENDS HERE—

BEST FRIENDS, I WOULD SAY!

OH, NO DOUBT. WHAT HAPPENED—

LOVERS, MAYBE?

TIME WILL TELL.

WHAT HAPPENED TO OUR OTHER FRIEND, BOGARD?

LET'S SEE...

OH, YES!

G'NASH ABDUCTIONS LLC.

WE WERE RETAINED TO DELIVER HIM TO...

THE BLACK SPIDER.

KRASH

REALLY?

I AM *NOT* FOND OF SPIDERS!!

WAIT A MO! BLACK SPIDER?

CLARENCE AND ENID SPIDER'S LITTLE BOY?

I DON'T—

KIDDING.

I DON'T KNOW ANYTHING ABOUT HIM. NEVER MET HIM.

SEE? WE WERE INSTRUCTED TO TURN MR. BOGARD OVER TO HIS REPRESENTATIVE. AND THAT'S WHAT WE DID.

COME ON, YA BIG BABY. I'LL PROTECT YOU FROM BUGS.

SPIDERS ARE NOT *BUGS!*

THEY'RE LITTLE HAIRY *TURDS* WITH LEGS.

G'NASH, OLD PAL, THIS HAS BEEN A SUPER GREAT TIME.

YES, IT HAS!

...EXCEPT FOR THE WHOLE PART WHERE I HAD TO SLAUGHTER ALL MY EMPLOYEES.

THEY WERE GOING TO MURDER *YOU!*

AND HEY— FEWER END-OF-YEAR BONUSES TO PAY OUT!

GOOD POINT!

CAN WE HAVE A HUG?

YOU KNOW, I JUST WATCHED YOU SQUISH A GERBLIN TO GUACAMOLE...AND THERE'S STILL SOME CHUNKS OF HIM... ON...YOU.

SO...

...PASS.

WILL ONE OF YOU GIVE ME JUST A QUICK HUG?

SOUNDS LIKE A JOB FOR...

MAGNUS!

HE *LOVES* HUGS! AND ANIMALS!

EXCEPT FOR THOSE OOKIE OLD SPIDERS!

SURE! FINE!

LET'S TURN THIS BUGBEAR...

...INTO A HUG-BEAR.

WHOOF!

HOLY SHIT...

HOLY SHIT...

HE IS IN *HORRIBLE* SHAPE!

OF COURSE, NOT EVERYBODY HAS THE STRENGTH OF COMMITMENT TO CARVE OUT AND KEEP A REALLY GREAT BOD.

...HEAL ME...

I THINK HE SAID "OIL CAN."

I'LL HEAL HIM.

YOU CAN'T! I'LL TAKE CARE OF IT WITH ONE OF OUR HEALING POTIONS.

WHY CAN'T I?

YOU ALREADY USED UP YOUR SPELL SLOTS!

WHAT THE HELL ARE SPELL SLOTS?!

OH, DEAR GOD...

THANK YOU, THANK YOU, GENTLE SOUL. I WILL NEVER FORGET THE KINDNESS YOU HAVE DONE FOR ME.

MY NAME IS BARRY J. BLUEJEANS, AND I AM READY TO KICK SOME GERBLIN ASS!

ALL THE ASSES THAT NEEDED TO BE KICKED HAVE BEEN KICKED, BAROLD.

YOU DIDN'T LEAVE ME *ONE* ASS?

THERE MAY BE A CHUNK OR TWO OF ASS OUTSIDE IN THE WEEDS YOU COULD KICK IF THAT WOULD MAKE YOU HAPPY.

OHHHH! NOW THE STUPID NAME MAKES MORE SENSE!

YEAH, WELL, NO SHIT. YOU THINK IT'S A *FAMILY NAME?*

OH, GREAT. HE'S A DOUCHE.

BARRY'S A DOUCHE.

TAKES ONE TO KNOW ONE.

MAY I SUGGEST WE GET THE HELL OUT OF HERE BEFORE THE SPELL WEARS OFF AND G'NASH BECOMES A LOT LESS CORDIAL?

WHAT THE HELL HAPPENED, BARRY?

A LOT OF SHIT.

AND IT WAS ALL REALLY TERRIBLE.

BOGARD TELLS ME THAT HIS TWO MORON BROTHERS—

HEY! THOSE ARE MY TWO MORON COUSINS YOU'RE TALKING ABOUT!

SORRY.

HE AND YOUR TWO MORON COUSINS FOUND A MAP LEADING TO...

THE LOST MINE of Haverdale.

WHY DIDN'T HE JUST *TELL* US THAT RIGHT UP FRONT?

WHY THE HELL WOULD HE TRUST YOU?

AGAIN: COUSINS?!

DWARVES HAVE, LIKE, *EIGHT HUNDRED* COUSINS!

YOU'RE BASICALLY PERFECT STRANGERS!

AND DATING'S A PAIN.

SO, BARRY.

THIS... BLACK SPIDER.

IS HE... YOU KNOW...

A *REAL* SPIDER? OR IS THAT...A NICK-NAME?

YOU KNOW, PUNKIN, SPIDERS ARE TEENSY-WEENSY THINGS.

NOT SURE HOW ONE WOULD BE ABLE TO KIDNAP A DWARF AND EXTORT AND SHIT.

I HAVE AN *ISSUE* WITH *SPIDERS!*

AND THINKING, APPARENTLY.

WHOEVER OR WHATEVER THE BLACK SPIDER IS, I AM ASSUMING THEY TOOK BOGARD TO FIND THE MINE LOCATION.

AFTER A GROUP OF ORC MARAUDERS TORE THROUGH IT, THE MINE WAS SHUT DOWN AND FORGOTTEN.

A LOT OF PEOPLE WOULD DO SOME PRETTY BAD SHIT TO FIND THAT MINE.

BUUUT—

—YOU DON'T KNOW WHERE THE MINE IS! SO WE CAN'T RESCUE HIM.

AWW, SHUCKS!

WELL, I GUESS WE SHOULD BE MOSEYIN' ON!

URK!

HANG ON.

WHY ALL THE FUSS ABOUT A PLAYED-OUT MINE?

IT'S NOT THE MINE...

IT'S THE VAULT *IN* THE MINE.

MINES? VAULTS?? WHY ARE WE LISTENING TO THIS HORSESHIT?

BOGARD SAYS THERE IS A VAULT DOWN THERE WITH TREASURES BEYOND BELIEF.

...POWERFUL WEAPONS...

...MYSTICAL ARTIFACTS...

...AND WEALTH BEYOND IMAGINING.

COME ON, FELLAS! THE MAN IS TRYING TO *TALK!* SHOW A LITTLE COURTESY.

ZOOM!

HUP

DO GO ON, DEAR, DEAR MR. BLUEJEANS.

WE CAN FIND THE MINE...

WITH THIS MAP!

TADAAA!

IT'S BLA-ANK.

NO SHI-IT.

HE'S A NU-UT.

NO HE'S NO-OT.

IT'S ENCHANTED!

I GUESS YOU COULD SAY THE REAL MAP—

...WAS IN*SIDE* THAT DAMNED DWARF!

LIKE, UP HIS BUTT?

EW, NO.

BOGARD'S BLOOD ACTIVATES THE MAP!

NOW THAT'S COOL...IF I SAY SO MYSELF.

AND FORTUNATELY, I ALSO HAVE—

A VIAL OF BOGARD'S BLOOD!!

WELL, YOU GOT THE "VIAL" PART RIGHT.

DAMN!!

DAMN, INDEED! I WAS HOPING TO SCORE SOME COOL WEAPON SHIT.

WELL!

THIS HAS BEEN A BLAST, FELLAS, BUT—

EXCUSE ME—

—WOULD A *COUSIN'S* BLOOD WORK?

WHAT A GOOD IDEA!

QUIT SQUIRMING!

I WOULD BE MORE COMFORTABLE IF YOU WOULD LET **ME** DECIDE WHERE MY BLOOD IS GOING TO BE COMING FROM!

WE JUST NEED TO MAKE SURE YOU GET A LOT OF BLOOD.

WHEN YOU SAY "A LOT"...

I THOUGHT YOU WERE SOME BIG, BRAVE HERO!

DOES WIDDLE MERLE-Y NEED SOMEBODY TO HOLD HIS HAND?

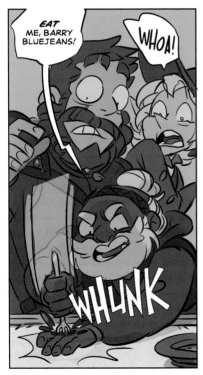

EAT ME, BARRY BLUEJEANS!

WHOA!

WHUNK

YOU SEE, **MISTER BLUEJEANS,** AS A CLERIC, I KNOW EVERY INCH OF MY ANATOMY.

THE BODY IS A VERY FAMILIAR ROADMAP TO ME.

I THINK YOU GOT A VEIN.

THAT IS QUITE A GUSHER.

WELL... YAY.

I'LL BE DAMNED! I DIDN'T THINK IT WOULD WORK!

SLURM SLURM SLURM

SLITHER

YOU DIDN'T THINK IT WOULD *WORK?!*

IT WAS A THEORY.

HERE!

THAT'S WHERE THEY MUST HAVE TAKEN BOGARD!

"CAVERN OF DANGLING DEATH"?

DOES *NOBODY* UNDERSTAND THE TOURISM INDUSTRY ANYMORE?

IT'S ABOUT A DAY'S RIDE FROM HERE. YOU CAN TAKE MY WAGON.

YOU'RE NOT GOING? WON'T IT BE BAD FOR YOUR BODYGUARD CAREER IF YOU DON'T SAVE YOUR CLIENT?

IT WILL BE *EQUALLY* BAD FOR MY CAREER IF I *JUST FUCKING DIE.*

Chapter 4

Chapter 5

TRY TO STAY POSITIVE. YOUR COUSINS COULD BE PERFECTLY FINE.

YEAH.

RIGHT.

...THANKS.

AW, *DAMMIT.*

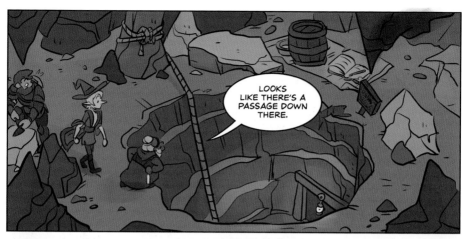

LOOKS LIKE THERE'S A PASSAGE DOWN THERE.

ARE THOSE NEW SHOES?

UHH... YEAH.

HAD TO CHANGE. MY DOGS WERE BARKING.

IT'S FUNNY.

THEY LOOK *JUST LIKE* THE MAGIC LOAFERS I GOT CAGGLE LAST CANDLENIGHTS.

WOW. SMALL WORLD.

WHAT ARE THE ODDS?

BLLÄP·BLRRT·
·BLIP·BLURT·

WHAT THE HELL IS *THAT?*

LET ME TAKE ANOTHER SHOT AT MY FOLEY WORK:

PLRRT·SQLPRT·

IT'S EITHER A DUCK OR SOMEBODY FARTING.

PLRRT·SQLPRT

MAYBE A FARTING DUCK?

I THINK IT'S GETTING CLOSER.

I DON'T KNOW— I PROBABLY NEED TO HEAR IT AGAIN TO BE SURE...

AWW, COME *ON,* GUYS!

"SPLORCH-SPLORCH-SPLORCH!"

THIS HAS TAKEN A REALLY GROSS TURN.

THERE'S ANOTHER CHAMBER RIGHT HERE. HOPEFULLY IT WILL BE LESS...SPLORCHY.

WHOEVER DESIGNED THESE CAVES HAD NO SENSE OF FENG SHUI!

HEY, TAAKO?

SHOULD I JUMP IN THIS SPRING?

IT'S ABOUT TEN STORIES DOWN, SO...YOU'D ALMOST CERTAINLY DIE.

YOUR CALL...

SPLORCH. SPLORCH SPLORCH

SNEAK SNEAK

THERE'S NOTHING LIKE COOL, CLEAR WATER, FILTERED THROUGH GOOD STONE.

I CAN'T WAIT TO TASTE IT.

SKRTT!

OOPS!

...YOUR OTHER COUSIN?

YEP. THAT'S DORB.

ARE YOU SURE?

POINT!

OH, DORB! YOU REALLY LOVED YOUR BEDAZZLER.

YOU AIN'T KIDDIN'.

HE JUST WANTED EVERYTHING TO BE SHINY AND PRETTY.

NICE JOB, DORB!

I'M SORRY FOR YOUR LOSS.

LET'S GET ROLLING!

JINGLE

HEY...DO YOU HAVE, LIKE, A **TON** OF COINS IN YOUR POCKET?

JINGLE! JINGLE! JINGLE!

NO! THEY'RE ALL BOTTLE CAPS! I'M SAVING THEM FOR UNICEF!

WELL, WHOEVER UNICEF IS, I'M SURE THEY'LL APPRECIATE THEM.

JUST BECAUSE WE'RE RISKING LIFE AND LIMB DOESN'T MEAN I LOSE THE SPIRIT OF GENEROSITY.

YOU SURE YOU DIDN'T FIND ANYTHING OVER THERE...?

JUST AN OLD, RUSTY KEY.

AN OLD, RUSTY KEY, ALL BY ITSELF!

AN OLD, RUSTY KEY.

JUST LAYING THERE. WEIRD, HUH?

CAN'T HELP BUT NOTICE THE ELEVATOR HAS AN OLD, RUSTY LOCK ON IT.

LET'S GET THE FUCK ON IT!

JINGLE!

SO WHAT KIND OF BOTTLE CAPS ARE WE TALKING AB—

THE CAPS ARE MY THING. LET IT GO.

STAND FAST, YOU IMPETUOUS SLAB OF BEEF!

MY *CLERIC-SENSES* TELL ME THERE ARE *MAGICAL PROPERTIES* IN THAT WATER!

GREAT! LET ME AT IT!

CLERIC-SENSES?

WELL, *I* WASN'T GONNA TRY IT FIRST. SHIT MIGHT BE POISON.

SLUUURRRP!

BAM

I AM *TOTALLY HEALED!*

IT'S AMAZING! I FEEL ENERGIZED! SEETHING WITH VITALITY!

LIKE A CIALIS COMMERCIAL!

EXACTLY!

I WONDER IF I CAN CONJURE UP A COUPLE OF BATHTUBS?

WE SHOULD ALL GET IN ON THIS SPRING!

UH-OHHH!!

YOU KNOW WHAT THAT MEANS!

SPRING BREAK!

LET'S GO SEE KENNY CHESNEY!

SP*LASH*

THAT'S WHO YOU WANNA SEE?

DWARVES HAVE VERY SPECIFIC MUSICAL TASTES!

MERLE, CAN WE ASSUME YOU WERE DRIVEN OUT OF YOUR DWARVEN CLAN BECAUSE OF YOUR LOVE FOR KENNY CHESNEY?

THEY'RE ALL SITTING AROUND, LISTENING TO SKRILLEX:

YEAH, MOST OF THEM ARE INTO, LIKE, EDM. THEY'RE CRAZY ABOUT DIPLO.

"WE'LL NEVER ACCEPT YOUR TASTE IN MUSIC, MERLE!"

"MAYBE SHE THINKS YOUR TRACTOR'S SEXY, BUT YOU ARE NO LONGER WELCOME HERE!"

Chapter 6

NOW WHAT YOU SEE HERE IS THE HEART OF THE MINING OPERATION.

HERE THEY WERE EXCAVATING THE MAGICAL ORE THEY WERE TURNING INTO POWERFUL WEAPONS.

PICTURE, IF YOU WILL, A WHOLE SHITLOAD OF ORCS RUSHING THROUGH THESE VERY CHAMBERS, HEADS SPINNING WITH TALES OF INCREDIBLE WEALTH!

AND BLADDERS BURSTING WITH PEE BECAUSE THEY HAD BEEN DRINKING A LOT AND THERE AREN'T A LOT OF REST STOPS ON THE ROAD FROM HAVERDALE.

IT SEEMS TO ME THAT THIS IS THE HEART OF THE MINING OPERATION WHERE THEY WERE EXCAVATING THE MAGICAL ORE FOR WEAPONS. I JUST FEEL IT IN MY BONES.

WE ALL HEARD HIM TOO, DUDE.

SO-O-O... HOW DOES EVERYBODY THINK THE ADVENTURE IS GOING?

B? MAYBE A SOLID B-?

WELCOME, EVERYBODY...

TO "TUNNEL TALK"!

SO, ARE YOU GUYS MORE DOG PEOPLE OR—

OKAY.

NO MORE TALKING AND SHARING!

I'M SORRY I STARTED THIS WHOLE THING.

HAVE I EVER TOLD YOU THE KEY TO CARVING THE PERFECT WOODEN DUCK?

THE SECRET IS SMALL, CONTROLLED STROKES!

OH, GOD!

HOW MUCH LONGER ARE WE GOING TO BE IN THIS CAVE?

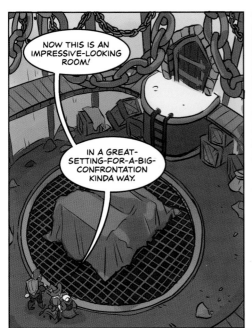

NOW THIS IS AN IMPRESSIVE-LOOKING ROOM!

IN A GREAT-SETTING-FOR-A-BIG-CONFRONTATION KINDA WAY.

I'M NOT 100% THIS THING CAN HOLD UP MY MUSCLE-Y MASSIVENESS.

IF IT CAN HOLD UP THIS BEAST—

—THEN I THINK WE'RE GOOD.

fWip!

K·R·A·M·SH

HEY!!

I DO THE KICKING DOORS OPEN AROUND HERE!

AHH, *SHIT.*

EASY, BOYS.

WE NEED TO EXHIBIT STRENGTH AND CONFIDENCE,

BUT WE DON'T WANT TO APPEAR TOO AGGRES—

WHAT'S SHAKIN'?

HAIL AND WELL MET!

—SIVE.

SHIT, SHIT, SHIT.

"HAIL AND WELL MET"? ARE YOU LITTLE JOHN NOW?

WELL, *YOU* SOUND LIKE FANTASY VINNIE BARBARINO!

JUST BE *QUIET* FOR A SECOND! GIVE ME A CHANCE TO *THINK!*

GREETINGS, FELLOW TRAVELER! I AM MAGNUS BURNSIDES, THE LEADER OF THIS STALWART GROUP, KNOWN AS "MAGNUS AND HIS MERRY MEN"—

ACTUALLY,

IT'S "TAAKO AND HIS TAAKETTES."

AS YOU MAY HAVE SURMISED, I AM THE TAAKO OF THAT TITLE—

MAY I SAY SOMETHING?

HAVE YOU HEARD THE WORD OF PAN TODAY?

MERLE'S WITNESSING.

YOU'RE SPREADING THE "GOOD NEWS OF PAN" *NOW*?!

WILL YOU THREE

JUST SHUT UP?!

I AM *VERY* BUSY RIGHT NOW. TRYING TO SAVE THE WORLD. I REALLY DON'T WANT TO TAKE THE TIME TO STOMP YOU INTO JELLY.

AT THE SAME TIME, I CAN'T HAVE YOU SCREWING UP MY MISSION, SO I'M TRYING TO FIGURE OUT WHAT TO DO WITH YOU.

LET'S PUT IT TO A VOTE:

ALL IN FAVOR OF THE NICE ORC LADY *NOT* EXTERMINATING US—

OKAY, SO.

YOU SEEM LIKE OKAY GUYS.

I'VE GOT A QUESTION FOR YOU.

WHAT HAPPENS NEXT DEPENDS ON HOW YOU ANSWER THIS QUESTION.

COOL! LIKE A "CHOOSE YOUR OWN ADVENTURE"!!

SURE—

—IF 90% OF THE PAGES READ "YOU DIED."

ARE YOU HERE

FOR

THE

AHHHAKSRNKYXX?!

WE DIDN'T QUITE CATCH THAT...?

DO YOU HAVE SOMETHING STUCK IN YOUR THROAT? LIKE A HAIR OR—?

ARE. YOU. HERE.

FOR.

THE.

...I THINK I GOT THIS.

WHY, NO, MA'AM!

WE'RE NOT SHAXS-RUHN-KICKS HUNTERS!

114

HE-E-E-L-P!

WHY SHOULD WE-E-E?

I COULD REALLY USE A HAND DOWN HERE!

WELL, *SURE!*

WHY *SHOULDN'T* WE HELP OUT THE NICE PERSON WHO LEFT US TO THE TENDER MERCIES OF A KILLER MULCHING MACHINE?

BE STALWART, WARRIOR WOMAN!

MAGNUS RUSHES IN. SO YOU ALL TAKE OFF RUNNING DOWN THE—

I DON'T.

WHAT?

NOT TO GO HELP SOMEONE WHO JUST *SICCED A METAL MURDER MACHINE ON US!!*

I'VE GOT THESE LITTLE STUBBY DWARF LEGS. I'M MORE OF A WADDLER, NOT A RUNNER.

GUYS!! GET IN HERE!!

AW, HELL. ALL RIGHT!

NOT ME!

YOU KNOW, THEY'RE JUST GOING TO GET SLAUGHTERED WITHOUT YOU THERE TO SAVE THEIR ASSES.

GOOD POINT.

ALL RIGHT. BUT I'M NOT RUNNING.

I WILL... MOSEY.

OH, VAT A FANTASTIC DEVELOPMENT!

VE HAFF GUESTS, MY DEAR! HOW EXCITING!

ALL RIGHT! THAT SOUNDS GOOD AND WEIRD!

I'M COMIN'!!

DO I NEED TO BE INTRODUCED? MY REPUTATION PRECEDES ME.

AND HERE IS MY SPIFFY SPIDER TABARD.

POINT
POINT
POINT

OHHHH!

YOU'RE THE *BLACK SPIDER!*

Black Spider
Race — DROW
Class WIZARD
+ PROFICIENCIES +
→ Black magic
→ Arachnid control
→ Bad accent

I HATE TO BE THAT GUY, BUT TECHNICALLY THAT'S A WHITE SPIDER.

SO, BLACK SPIDER—

ZAT'S ACTUALLY JUST AN ALIAS, NOT MY REAL NAME.

LISTEN, MERLE, I KNOW HOW THIS WORKS!

IF WE FIGURE OUT HIS NAME, HE'S BANISHED.

HE'S NOT *BEETLEJUICE*.

IT'S BRIAN. MAGIC BRIAN.

NOW IT IS MY TURN TO ASK A QUESTION.

Black Spider
Alias: Brian (Magic)

HOW THE *FUCK* DO YOU KNOW ABOUT THIS MAGICAL MINE...

...OF...

...UH...

...MINE?

BELIEVE IT OR NOT... CRAIGSLIST?

VELL, I *DON'T* BELIEVE IT.

I THINK YOU ARE HERE FOR THE ＡＳＨＨＨＨＸＦＲＮＫＹＸＸ

N...NO?

LOOK, BRIAN—MAY I CALL YOU BRI?

BRI-BRI, WE'RE BOTH MAGIC DUDES. CAN YOU EXPLAIN WHY OCCASIONALLY WHEN YOU TALK—IN YOUR *TRULY* MELLIFLUOUS VOICE, I MUST ADD—WE JUST HEAR STATIC?

PERHAPS...THE REASON YOU CAN'T HEAR IT VEN I SAY ＳＨＨＸＸＸ IS BECAUSE ＳＨＺＺＰＨＺＸＸ AND YOU ACTUALLY ＳＨＦＺＨ SO YOU WON'T BE ABLE TO UNDERSTAND THIS ＳＨＲＺ?

SCREW THAT NOISE! I'M HERE FOR MY COUSIN!!

VICH COUSIN?

OH, VELL, I SUPPOSE IT VOULD HAVE TO BE...

THE ONLY SURVIVING ONE?

HIS *NAME*... IS...*BOGARD*.

UH... OF COURZE, OF COURZE! BOGARD!

GOODNESS, AREN'T YOU AN ANGRY LITTLE FELLOW.

YOU MAY MOST CERTAINLY TAKE... BOGARD. TAKE HIM AND GO.

EXCELLENT! PLEASURE DOING BUSINESS WITH YOU!

OH!

I DO NEED ONE MORE THING...

...A TINY BIT MORE OF HIS BLOOD.

LET ME AT HIM!!

THAT'S NOT GOING TO WORK FOR US.

126

WHO DIDN'T SEE *THAT* COMING?

ME.

OKAY...

I SEE WHAT HE'S TRYING TO DO HERE!

I'M THE *REAL* BOGARD!

I CAN TELL YOU ANYTHING YOU WANT TO KNOW ABOUT MYSELF! MY CLAN! ANYTHING!

YOU HAVE TO BELIEVE ME!

WOOP!

OH NOOO!

YOU HAFF SOLVED MY FINAL RIDDLE!

YOU HAVE PROVEN YOURSELVES TO BE QUITE THE ADVENTURERS...

YOU MUST BE DECLARED ZE RIDDLE MASTERS...

BLURRK

OH, I'VE LANDED ON BRYAN...

HE VASN'T AS SOFT AS I WOULD HAVE IMAGINED... DIDN'T REALLY BREAK MY FALL ALL ZAT MUCH...

I THINK I AM DOING THE DYING NOW...ZE LIFE IS FLAGGING FROM MY BODY...

OH! I SEE MY FAMILY—

WHAMSH

...

PHEW.

143

Chapter 7

I CANNOT **BELIEVE** YOU GUYS AREN'T TOTALLY DEAD!

MAGIC BRIAN IS ONE OF THE MOST ACCOMPLISHED, POWERFUL WIZARDS I HAVE EVER ENCOUNTERED!

I AM FLABBERGASTED, FRANKLY, THAT WE ALL DID NOT PERISH!

YOU'RE... WELCOME... I GUESS?

WE'RE PRETTY MUCH RAD.

IF YOU'LL EXCUSE ME, I NEED TO RECOVER SOMETHING VERY QUICKLY.

NONE OF YOU LEAVE!!

HOLD UP, HOLD UP!

BEFORE YOU GO **ANYWHERE**,

WHAT THE **HELL** IS THIS ALL ABOUT?!

I PROMISE:

I WILL TELL YOU

AS SOON AS I AM *LITERALLY ABLE TO.*

LISTEN. I HAVE A LITTLE BIT OF MAGICAL EXPERTISE.

I ASSUME THIS STATIC SHIT WHEN YOU TALK IS SOME SORT OF...CURSE?

PREVENTING FURTHER DISCUSSION FROM TAKING PLACE?

YOU ASSUME WRONG...

DONK

...SUPER DUPER WRONG.

...

...SLOW-FALL SPELL.

YEAH, GUESSED THAT.

REEEALLY SLOW-FALL SPELL.

KINDA ANTI-CLIMACTIC, BUT WHATEV.

A-F-K!

AWESOME... FLAMING... KOBOLDS?

ANGRY.... FIGHTERS... KILL?

AWAY FLOATS KILLIAN.

UHN...

HOW ARE YOU FEELING?

WELL, I SMOKE THREE PACKS A DAY. I DRINK A SIX-PACK A DAY, AND THEN EAT THE BOTTLES. I'VE BEEN EATING INSULATION FOR YEARS...

THAT'S NOT GOOD.

YEAH, I'M REAL FUCKED UP OVER HERE.

Bogard Stoneseeker

Race DWARF
Class ENGINEER

+ PROFICIENCIES +
→ Mining
→ Ancestry
→ Plot point-ing

I CAN'T BELIEVE LIL COUSIN MERLEY AND HIS PALS SAVED ME FROM *MAGIC BRIAN!*

WHY IS EVERYBODY SO SHOCKED?

WHERE'S BARRY, BY THE WAY?

OH, HE'S GOOD.

HANGING OUT BACK AT THE BAR.

HE SAID HE HAD TO WAIT FOR HIS ORDER OF CHICKEN WINGS AND THEN HE'D MEET RIGHT UP WITH US.

HAH! TYPICAL BARRY!

SO, LITTLE DUDE... WHY *WAS* MAGIC BRIAN WANTING ALL YOUR BLOOD?

COME ON AND I'LL SHOW YOU.

ALL RIGHT, YOU GUYS DESERVE SOME ANSWERS—

YES!

RIGHT.

AND SOME MONEY.

MY FATHER—

WAIT!

HOLD ON A SECOND!

I THINK IT'S IMPORTANT TO GET THE TRUTH OUT OF MY COUSIN HERE.

YOU WANNA BEAT IT OUT OF HIM?

NO!!

I HAVE A THING CALLED...

...ZONE OF TRUTH!

SUUURE YOU DO.

NO, NO— IT'S A GREAT IDEA.

GO FOR IT!

IT WOULD BE AWESOME IF ONE OF US COULD CAST SOME KIND OF LIGHT SPELL...

NO SHIT.

HE MEANS YOU.

SNAP!

LAVENDER. VERY CALMING.

PLINK

IT'S LIKE...

...BLACK GLASS...?

PLINK
PLINK

SOMETHING'S NOT RIGHT.

NO SHIT, GENIUS.

BRO!!!

I WON'T LEAVE YOU HANGING!

FWASH!!

GOOD GOING, DIPSHIT.

THAT'S ABOUT THREE DAMAGE.

TOTALLY WORTH IT.

NO, NO, NO, NO, *NO!!*

SO THE DWARF-SHAPED CHARCOAL BRIQUETTE? HIS FATHER, RIGHT?

YEP, THAT'S GOTTA BE MY UNCLE.

HE DOESN'T SEEM REAL TORN UP ABOUT IT.

!!

MY FAMILY IS PRETTY FUCKED UP.

THIS VAULT IS SUPPOSED TO BE FILLED WITH MAGICAL WEAPONS AND ARMAMENTS!

WHERE IS ALL OF IT?! I DON'T UNDERSTAND!!

HEY, HEY, CALM DOWN THERE, BUCKO—

WHAT

DID I

TELL YOU?!

NUDGE NUDGE NUDGE

I **TOLD** YOU GUYS TO STAY PUT!

WE GOT BORED! YOU WERE GONE FOR FOUR HOURS!

IT WAS LIKE A **MINUTE** AND A **HALF!!**

WHY DO YOU NOT **LISTEN** TO ME?!

OH, NO...

NONE OF YOU TRIED TO HIGH-FIVE THAT THING, DID YOU?!

ARE WE STILL IN THE TRUTH CIRCLE THING?

NO, THAT WAS BACK IN THE OTHER ROOM.

THEN...

NO.

GOD, NO!

YOU'D HAVE TO BE A **COMPLETE IDIOT** TO HIGH-FIVE THAT THING!

WELL, I DON'T KNOW ABOUT **THAT.**

ARE YOU GUYS HERE WITH THIS FILTHY ORC?

WHOA! HEY!

LET'S CHEESE IT WITH THE RACISM, BOGIE!

DID YOU JUST CALL ME... "FILTHY"?

COME ON, NOW! LET'S BUILD BRIDGES, NOT WALLS!

OKAY, BOGIE, WHY DON'T YOU DIAL DOWN THE HATE A TAD...

...AND LET ME HAVE THE GAUNTLET.

THIS GAUNTLET AND EVERYTHING IN THIS VAULT IS MY BIRTHRIGHT! THERE'S *NO WAY* I AM GIVING THIS THING UP TO *YOU!*

DOOOOOON'T TEST ME! I HAVE HAD A *REALLY* LONG DAY! I GOT ALL WEBBED UP IN THAT OTHER ROOM, AND I HATED THAT!

BOYS, YOU'VE SERVED ME WELL. I HAVE ONE LAST JOB FOR YOU...

I NEED YOU TO TAKE HER OUT.

NOBODY IS TAKING ANYBODY OUT!

COUNT TO TEN OR SOMETHING!

BOGARD, DO YOU KNOW WHY THIS ROOM IS EMPTY AND THERE'S A GAUNTLET ON THAT DUDE'S HAND?

"THAT DUDE" WAS MY *FATHER!* AND NO, I DON'T KNOW WHY IT'S THE ONLY THING IN THE VAULT—

BUT I KNOW THAT IT'S *MINE!*

KILLIAN, DO *YOU* KNOW WHAT THAT THING IS?

I HAVE A *PRETTY GOOD GODDAMN IDEA,* YEAH.

THAT IS THE *WHOLE REASON* I WAS *SENT* HERE! TO STOP MAGIC BRIAN FROM GETTING THE *SHKXXX*

SEE, IT KIND OF SOUNDS LIKE SOMEONE FRYING BACON WHILE PLAYING THE MARACAS.

I WOULD *KILL* FOR SOME BACON RIGHT NOW.

TELL ME ABOUT IT.

167

THAT WENT

ABOUT AS SHITTY

AS IT POSSIBLY COULD HAVE GONE.

WHAT ARE YOU TALKING ABOUT?! I ALMOST HAD HIM!

OF COURSE YOU DID, KITTEN.

LISTEN.

I'VE GOT TO STOP HIM BEFORE HE DESTROYS THE *WHOLE WORLD.*

AND I'M GOING TO NEED YOUR HELP TO DO IT.

Chapter 8

IT LOOKS LIKE BOGARD HAS HAD A BUSY DAY!

SCARES BUNNIES

UPSETS A BARD

BURNS UP CORNFIELD

HEADS TOWARD TOWN

DRIES UP POND

SO, BOGARD: STILL BURNING...

THIS WAY TO HAVERDALE

★ YEARS ★ SINCE LAST DESTRUCTION

I'M TELLING YOU, HE'S GOING AFTER BARRY BLUEJEANS!

WHY? TO INCINERATE HIM?

BOGARD MAY BE AN ASSHOLE, BUT HE'S STILL FAMILY! I WANT TO STOP HIM BEFORE HE HURTS HIMSELF OR ANYONE ELSE!

UHH...

I THINK THAT SHIP DONE SAILED.

HE MAY BE A THREE-ALARM HATE-MONGER, BUT HE SEEMS TO HAVE A HEALTHY RESPECT FOR ARCHITECTURE. THESE BUILDINGS ARE UNTOUCHED.

SLAM!

SHUT

EXCEPT FOR THAT ONE.

THAT'S OUR BARRY!

AHHH!

I'M RUSHING IN!

GOTTA LOVE HIS CONSISTENCY, AT LEAST.

AHHH! FWOOSH

OH MY GOD!!

IT'S YOU GUYS!!

HOW ARE YOU NOT *DEAD?!*

CAREFUL! THAT'S COUTURE, MY DUDE!

YOU GUYS HAVE TO HELP ME!! I'VE NEVER SEEN HIM LIKE THIS!

YOU MEAN ENGULFED IN FLAMES AND ALL MAGICAL AND SHIT?

WELL, THAT, AND HOW BIZARRE HE'S ACTING!

LIKE, HE'S NOT KNOWN FOR HIS CALM DEMEANOR, BUT I'VE NEVER SEEN HIM GET *THIS* PISSED.

BRUSH
BRUSH

LISTEN TO ME...

BOGARD, LISTEN! THAT GAUNTLET IS CONSUMING YOU!

REMEMBER YOUR FATHER IN THE VAULT!

IF YOU DON'T REMOVE THE GLOVE, YOU ARE GOING TO DIE!

I CAN... CONTROL IT.

YOU CAN'T!

LOOK AT YOURSELF! THIS ISN'T LIKE YOU!

HAH!!

YOU DON'T KNOW WHAT I'M LIKE!!

I DO.

SHE WAS RUN OVER BY A MANURE CART WHILE SHE WAS CROSSING THE STREET TO BUY SMOKES!

MAYBE AN ORC WAS DRIVING!

HEE-HEE!!

SORRY!

SORRY!

IS THIS WHAT SHE WOULD HAVE WANTED?

WOULD SHE HAVE WANTED YOU TO KILL ALL THESE INNOCENT FOLKS? AND BURN YOUR OWN ASS UP AT THE SAME TIME?

I DON'T THINK SO.

SHE LOVED YOU AN AWFUL LOT.

183

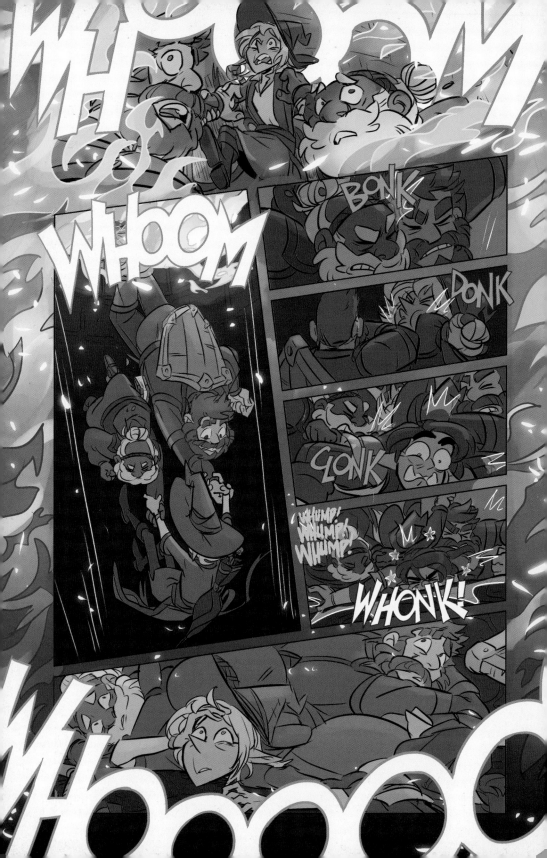

Chapter 9

SO...

HERE WE ARE AT THE BOTTOM OF A WELL.

I GUESS WE JUST...

...LIVE DOWN HERE NOW?

UNLESS EITHER OF YOU CLOWNS KNOWS HOW TO FLY.

IS KILLIAN... DEAD?

JUST KNOCKED OUT, I THINK.

OF COURSE...

THAT MAY BE BECAUSE WE CRASHED INTO HER.

IT WAS HER DUMB IDEA TO DIVE INTO A WELL.

THAT'S TRUE. THIS IS ON HER.

AND SO ARE WE.

SNRK

SNRK

PFFT

HA HA HA HA HA HA HA HA HA HA HA

YOU KNOW, BOYS...

I'M STARTING TO THINK WE MAY SUCK AT THIS.

YOU DO... REALIZE...THAT BASICALLY...I AM HAULING...EVERYBODY... UP THIS WELL... RIGHT?

WE FIGURED YOU HAD A PROFICIENCY IN WELL-HAULING.

COME TO THINK OF IT...

...I BELIEVE I DO.

CAN WE CUT DOWN ON THE CHITCHAT JUST A *SMIDGE* SO MAYBE I COULD CONCENTRATE ON MAKING THIS DAMN THING WORK?

YOU LOOK LIKE A MEDIEVAL MARY POPPINS!!

SPIT-SPOT, LET'S GET CLIMBING.

NEVER MIND NOW! WE'RE—

THERE'S NOTHING LEFT.

LOOK, I'VE HAD TO LEAVE TOWNS IN A HURRY BEFORE.

IT'S NEVER UNFIXABLE.

WE'LL TAKE UP A COLLECTION AND IF THE VILLAGERS DIG DEEP ENOUGH INTO THEIR POCKETS FOR THE REBUILDING FUND I'M SURE—

...EVERYTHING'S GONE.

EVERY**BODY'S** GONE!

WHAT THE FUCK *IS* THAT THING?

KILLIAN MUST KNOW SOMETHING ABOUT IT, RIGHT? SHE SAID SHE WAS SENT HERE BECAUSE OF IT.

SO THE ONE PERSON WHO COULD HANDLE THE GAUNTLET IS ASLEEP.

NOT ASLEEP. SHE'S UNCONSCIOUS. SHE'S NOT WAKING UP ANYTIME SOON.

SO...WHAT DO WE DO?

COULD WE CUT OFF BOGARD'S ARM?

WHAT KIND OF MONSTER *ARE* YOU?

WE KNOW TOUCHING THE GLOVE FROM THE OUTSIDE IS NOT GOOD. AND PUTTING IT ON IS *REALLY* STUPID.

UNLESS...

...UNLESSSSS...

WHAT IF ONE OF US JUST NEEDS TO CONTROL IT BETTER THAN BOGARD DID?

"ONE OF US," HUH...

YOU. HE MEANS YOU.

I'M NOT GETTING MY ASS BLASTED OFF AGAIN.

IF THIS WORKS, I'M PAWNING THE HELL OUT OF IT.

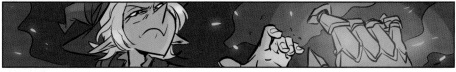

HI THERE, TAAKO!

I WAS THINKING WE MIGHT WANT TO BE FRIENDS!

NOT ONLY AM I *SEETHING* WITH MYSTICAL ENERGY, BUT YOU *KNOW* I WOULD LOOK *AMAZING* ON YOU!

WHAT DO YOU SAY, PAL?

kkssXXkkkxss
Gauntlet
Power Level:
Off the charts, baby
Weakness:
A bit chatty

NOPE!

I HATE NEEDY ACCESSORIES.

CHECK THIS OUT.

I CAST *SENSE MECHANISM!*

YOU DON'T KNOW HOW TO DO THAT.

NO, I DON'T.

THAT'S IT. I'M GONNA TRY AND WAKE HER UP. MAYBE I HAVE AN ANTI-CONCUSSION SPELL OR SOMETHING.

I THINK IT'S MY LAST SPELL SLOT.

OH, LIKE YOU'VE REALLY BEEN KEEPING TRACK OF THAT!!

LET'S DO ONE THING FIRST.

BLINK BLINK

DID...DID WE SAVE... HAVERDALE?

NOT SO MUCH.

I'M PRETTY SURE I'M GOING TO NEED MY CROSSBOW.

OH.

AND I'M PRETTY SURE I NEED YOU TO UNTIE ME.

AND WE'RE "PRETTY SURE" WE COULD HAVE DONE A LOT MORE FOR HAVERDALE...

IF WE HAD KNOWN WHAT THE *FUCK* WAS GOING ON!

HOW MANY TIMES DO I HAVE TO TELL YOU THAT I *LITERALLY!!*

CAN'T TELL YOU!!

ANYTHING!!

I BET YOU COULD HAVE TOLD US A *LIIIITTLE* BIT MORE.

A COUPLE OF CONTEXT CLUES! DRAW A PICTURE! CHARADES!

MAYBE DROP THE *HINT* THAT BOGARD COULD *POSSIBLY* TURN INTO A GIANT MADE OUT OF FIRE.

ALL RIGHT! *ALL RIGHT!*

I WILL HAVE TO CHOOSE MY WORDS VERY CAREFULLY, BUT I WILL TELL YOU WHAT I CAN...

...AS SOON AS YOU...?

HOW DO I SAY THIS...

I AM AN... EMPLOYEE... OF A GROUP OF...UM...

...CONCERNED PEOPLE.

HOW WE DOING SO FAR?

SO FAR, SO GOOD. NO CRACKLING.

THESE ...INDIVIDUALS... ARE WANTING...TO SKRKXXX

YEP, THERE WE GO! CRACKLES! WE GOT CRACKLES!!

DAMMIT!

THESE INDIVIDUALS WANT...TO DO A GOOD THING. MAKE...THE WHOLE WORLD...SAFER.

HOW'S THAT?

THAT WAS PRETTY CLEAR.

IT'S JUST A LITTLE HARD TO BUY BECAUSE THE FIRST TIME WE MET YOU...

YOU SENT A GIANT GRINDER THING NAMED LOUISE TO SQUASH US!!

I TOLD HER NON-LETHAL PARAMETERS!!

I THOUGHT YOU WERE TRYING TO STOP MY GROUP OF PEOPLE FROM...DOING THAT GOOD THING!

IS THAT BRACER THE REASON YOU CAN'T TELL US ABOUT THE GAUNTLET?

THIS OLD THING?

NOOOO!

WAIT!

THE GAUNTLET...

HOW HAVE NONE OF YOU PICKED UP THE GAUNTLET AND PUT IT ON??

OH, WE'RE SUPER COOL.

YEAH, WE'RE REALLY CHILL.

I'M TOO SHORT TO REACH IT.

IT TALKED TO ME. IN MY NOODLE.

IT WANTED ME TO PUT IT ON, BUT IT WAS SO DAMNED PUSHY.

HONESTLY, I WAS A LITTLE AFRAID, IF WE'RE JUST PUTTING IT OUT THERE.

YOU MEAN, YOU DIDN'T SUCCUMB TO ITS THRALL?

I THINK I WOULD KNOW IF I WAS THRALL-ED... SO...NO?

WHERE DID YOU GUYS *COME* FROM?

I HAIL FROM THE PICTURESQUE TOWN OF—

ENOUGH WITH THE BACKSTORY!

IF YOU THREE WERE ABLE TO ESCAPE THE THRALL OF THAT THING...

...I THINK WE COULD USE PEOPLE LIKE YOU!

WHO'S "WE"?

"CAUSE IT FEELS JUST LIKE I'M WALKIN' ON BROKEN GLAAAASS..."

FIRST KENNY CHESNEY, NOW ANNIE LENNOX?

DUDE! YOU'RE KILLIN' IT!

SO ARE THERE, LIKE, BODIES OR SKELETONS OR SOME SHIT LIKE THAT IN THE GLASS?

NO.

GOOD. BECAUSE THAT WOULD BE NASTY.

NO, THEY WERE PROBABLY VAPORIZED.

INSTANTLY.

GREAT.

DO YOU THINK WE SHOULD...

I DON'T KNOW...

...SAY SOMETHING?

AHEM

OH LOVING AND POWERFUL PAN!

PLEASE BE WITH THESE POOR SOULS!

GUIDE THEM ON THEIR JOURNEY TO A BETTER PLACE!

AND PLEASE DON'T BLAME US FOR ANY OF THIS SHIT.

AMEN.

I FEEL BAD ABOUT BARRY BLUEJEANS.

ME, TOO.

MAYBE I COULD COME UP WITH A SON...

"BARRY JORTS"!

WE HAD SOME REAL MERCHANDISING OPPORTUNITIES WITH THAT CHARACTER.

OKAY, THIS OUGHT TO BE GOOD.

CLICK

JUST SORT OF WAITING FOR APPROVAL HERE.

SHOULDN'T TAKE TOO LONG.

SCRITCH SCRATCH

SO...

WHAT ARE YOUR NAMES AGAIN?

I AM, OF COURSE, MAGNUS BURNSIDES.

OF COURSE. AND YOU ARE—?

—ALSO KNOWN AS "THE HAMMER."

"THE HAMMER"?

I PICKED UP A NICKNAME A COUPLE OF DAYS AGO.

WHILE WE HAVE BEEN ON THIS LITTLE ADVENTURE...YOU PICKED UP A NICKNAME.

WHO GAVE IT TO YOU?

NOT IMPORTANT.

MY FAMILY DIDN'T HAVE A LOT OF MATERIAL POSSESSIONS, BUT WE HAD AN ABUNDANCE OF LO—

I'LL REMEMBER THAT.

SO, TAAKO—

LIFE IN RAVEN'S ROOST WAS SIMPLE—

PAN, KILL ME.

BUT FOR A LAD WITH A HEART FOR ADVENTURE—

WHAT IS **WRONG** WITH THIS THING? IT NEVER TAKES THIS LONG.

THERE WE GO!! CONNECTION!!

I'LL HURRY.

LIFEINRAVENS ROOSTWASSIMPLEBUT FORALADWITH—

TO BE CONTINUED, PUNKIN.

Chapter 10

I BET WE STEER IT WITH OUR BRAINS! DO WE?

IT'LL BE OKAY. COME ON...

LOOK HOW SMALL IT IS.

LOOKS HUGE TO LITTLE OLE ME.

OKAY, SO LIKE, I'M A LITTLE BIT SCARED.

IT'LL BE FUN! NOT A THING TO BE SCARED OF.

HEY, GUYS! I THINK WE STEER IT WITH OUR BRAINS!

HA HA!

MAYBE ONE THING TO BE SCARED OF.

SORRY, HAVERDALE.

THIS IS SOOOO COOL!

YOU GUYS ARE GOING TO LOVE WHAT HAPPENS NEXT.

OPEN THE
PORTHOLE.

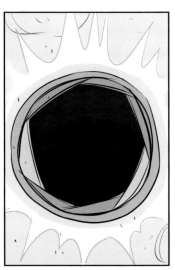

WELL,
GUYS...

...HOLD
ON TO YOUR
BUTTS.

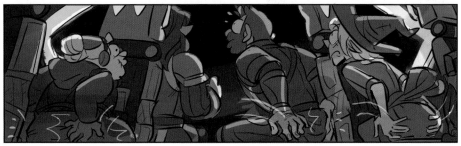

SHUT.

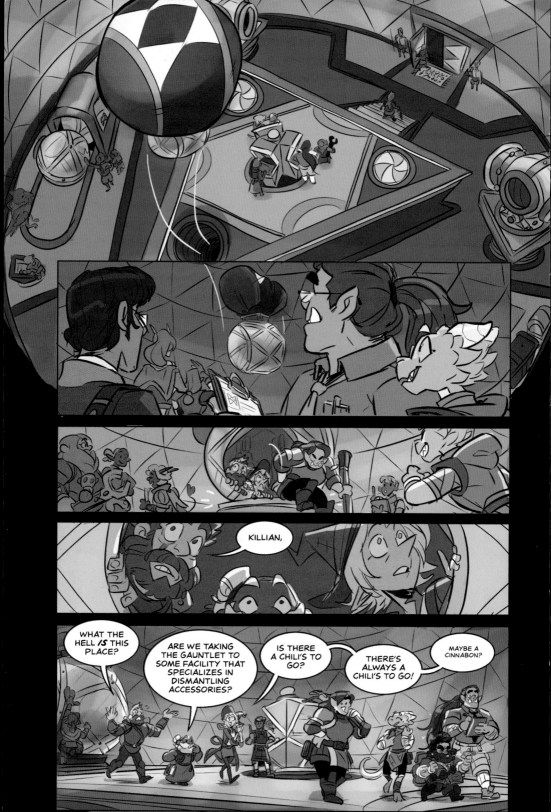

HANG ON A SECOND. I'M FEELING KIND OF SHITTY.

YEAH, ME, TOO. I DON'T WANT TO PUKE ON THIS ROBE.

OH, DAMN! I KNOW WHAT HAPPENED! WE DIED IN THE EXPLOSION IN HAVERDALE AND THIS IS PURGATORY!!

THIS IS NOT PURGATORY.

THAT'S WHAT THEY ALWAYS SAY...

IT'S NOT PURGATORY!

DON'T TELL US WHAT IT ISN'T...TELL US WHAT IT ISN'T-N'T!

YEAH, I THINK IT'S TIME FOR YOU TO FESS UP. WHO'S GONNA GET RID OF THE MURDER GLOVE?

WHAT MY COLLEAGUES ARE TRYING TO SAY IS: *WHAT THE FUCK?*

OKAY... FINE!

I AM TAKING YOU TO SEE SKRKX

SHE WILL HAVE SKXX PUT THE GAUNTLET INTO THE SKRKX WHICH WILL SKXXSS

AND THEN SHE WILL PROBABLY INVITE YOU TO BECOME SAK FOR THE XXXSI!!

THAT'S "THE FUCK"!

HAPPY???!!

I'M DOING OKAY, I GUESS.

I WILL BE RIGHT BACK, BUT PLEASE—

moon sweet moon

PLEASE! FOR *ONCE!* STAY HERE AND

DON'T

MESS

SHIT

UP!

MAN, IF I FELT JUST A LITTLE LESS CRUMMY I WOULD GO OUT AND MESS SHIT UP ON PURPOSE.

YOU GUYS WANT TO COP A SQUAT?

YEAH, LET'S JUST CHILL.

SO, MAGNUS, YOU WANNA TAKE A MINUTE? SHARE? MAYBE TELL US THAT EPIC MAGNUS BACKSTORY?

YOU KNOW WHAT? I DON'T FEEL LIKE IT RIGHT NOW.

YOU REALLY *ARE* SICK.

HEY, YOU GUYS WANNA TRY—

—A LITTLE SIP—

—OF... THIS?

gulp

gulp

gulp

TASTES LIKE GO-GURT.

IT'S NOT GO-GURT, IT'S BRANDY.

WELL, SOMEBODY SOLD YOU GO-GURT-FLAVORED BRANDY.

THIS STUFF WILL MAKE YOU FEEL A LITTLE BETTER. HELPS WITH THE DISORIENTATION A BIT.

gulp

HEY, DON'T BOGART THE GO-GURT.

I KNOW THINGS ARE GONNA BE PRETTY CONFUSING FOR A WHILE, WHAT WITH THE ░KKKK░ GOING ON AND THE DIZZINESS.

IF IT MAKES YOU FEEL BETTER, EVERYBODY HERE AT ░KGAXXKRSS░ WENT THROUGH THE SAME THING, SO DON'T WORRY.

IT'S GONNA GET A LOT BETTER SOON, AND WE'RE ALL REALLY, REALLY EXCITED TO HAVE YOU JOIN ░KRXX░.

DO WE KNOW THIS GUY?

SORRY! MY NAME'S AVI!

OKAY, YOU GUYS ARE CLEAR! JUST FOLLOW ME AND WE'LL GET THIS SHOW ON THE ROAD.

CLAP

WAIT...

...I THINK I KNOW THIS ONE!

...TALL AND TAN AND YOUNG AND LOVELY...

...THE GIRL FROM IPANEMA GOES WALKING....

...AND WHEN SHE PASSES, EACH ONE SHE PASSES GOES...

AAAHHHHH!

AUGH

DING!

THIS IS AN AWFUL LOT OF GUARDS...

...AND AN AWFUL LOT OF WEAPONRY.

I LIKE THEIR HATS!

WHSSK!

SKKXXXKS IS WAITING FOR THEM.

THANK YOU, JOHANN.

YEAH, WHATEVER.

ALL RIGHT. LISTEN, GUYS... THIS IS AS FAR AS I CAN GO.

BUT—

~SKXXXR~ WILL ANSWER ALL YOUR QUESTIONS. TAKE THE ~SKX~ TO HER AND SHE WILL DEAL WITH IT.

I WILL SEE YOU LATER—

—I SINCERELY HOPE.

GEEZ. OMINOUS MUCH?

WELL, FELLAS. THIS IS IT! THE BIG MOMENT.

WE DON'T KNOW WHAT'S ON THE OTHER SIDE OF THIS DOOR.

WE DON'T KNOW WHO THESE PEOPLE ARE OR WHAT THE HELL THEY'RE DOING.

BUT FOR THE TIME BEING, WE SEEM TO BE TANGLED UP IN THIS "TEAM," SO I SUPPOSE WE HAVE TO START MAKING DECISIONS TOGE—

WSSK!

HE WALKED THROUGH THE DOOR, DIDN'T HE?

OF COURSE HE DID.

DO YOU GUYS SEE THIS?

EVERY TIME I LOOK AT IT, IT'S LIKE I'M LOOKING AWAY FROM IT.

WHAT IS THAT *SOUND?*

IT'S LIKE A CAT TRYING TO YODEL.

I'VE NEVER HEARD IT DESCRIBED LIKE THAT, BUT YOU'RE—

...NOT...

...ENTIRELY...

...WRONG...

MA'AM? ARE YOU OKAY?

...YES! OF COURSE!

DAVENPORT!!

TAP TAP TAP

WHAT DO YOU EXPECT US TO DO WITH THIS VILE-LOOKING SHIT?

I EXPECT YOU TO DRINK IT.

ARE YOU TRYING TO KILL US?

NO.

BELIEVE IT OR NOT...

I'M TRYING TO HIRE YOU.

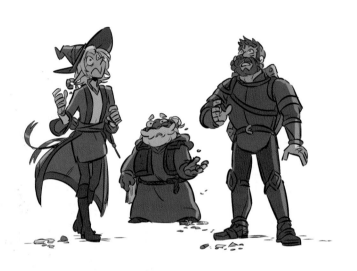

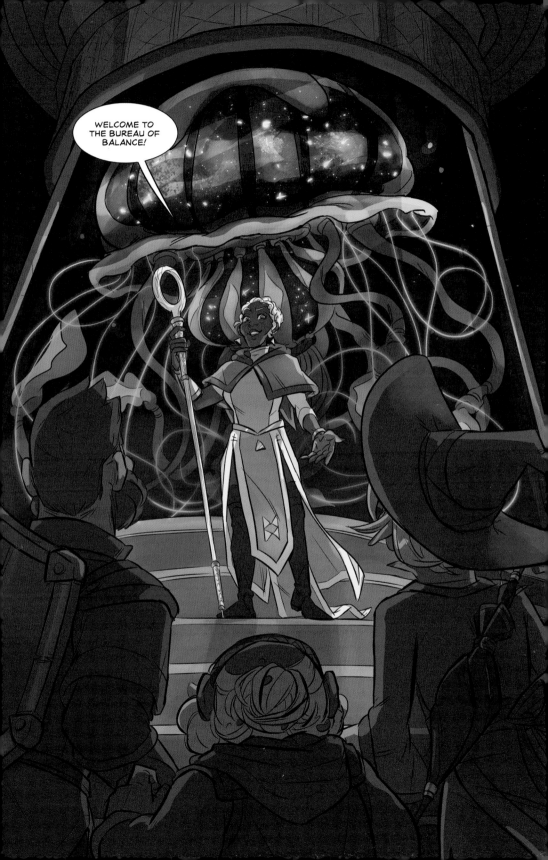

The ADVENTURE CONTINUES in

Coming Soon!

Fan Art Gallery

The *Adventure Zone* has been lucky enough to garner a passionate and deeply creative fandom. Many thanks to the fan artists who contributed pieces to this gallery—and to all the writers, artists, creators, and fans of all stripes who have made *The Adventure Zone* what it is.

THE
ADVENTURE ZONE
Basic Game Adventure
Here There Be Gerblins

Chris Kindred

Liz Parlett

Sebastián "Seb" Jimenez

Mickey Quinn

Mu X. Jones

Johanna The Mad

Adrienne Valdes